The Great Toronto Bicycling Guide

Elliott Katz

Illustrated by Leong Leung

Great North Books

ISBN 0-920361-01-3
Copyright © 1985, 1987 by Elliott Katz
Revised edition 1987.

Illustration and design: Leong Leung
Thanks to Gary Bradski for his assistance.
Printed in Canada

Third printing.

Published by:
Great North Books
P.O. Box 507, Station Z
Toronto, Ontario, Canada M5N 2Z6

Trade distribution by:
Firefly Books Ltd.
3520 Pharmacy Avenue, Unit 1-C
Scarborough, Ontario, Canada M1W 2T8

Contents

Two roads diverged in a wood and I —
I took the one less travelled by,
And that has made all the difference.
— Robert Frost

Introduction

Cycling along scenic bicycle pathways is one of the joys of living in or visiting Toronto. On a bicycle you have the freedom to explore peaceful wooded valleys, picturesque riverbanks, tree-framed creeks or the beautiful Lake Ontario shoreline. You're travelling slow enough to hear the birds, smell the forest and absorb the tranquility of Toronto's natural areas; yet going fast enough to feel the exhilaration of the wind blowing in your face. A bicycle ride is an enjoyable outing to share with friends or with your family. Most routes have picnic tables and some even have barbecues. Bicycling is also great exercise.

This book is your guide to enjoying Toronto's best off-street bicycle paths. Each route description includes how to reach the start of the trail by bicycle, car or subway. It guides you along the path, pointing out details of the area's history and wildlife, and tells you how to get back from the end of the route. Detailed, easy-to-read maps accompany each route description. Don't let this book sit on the shelf. Get on your bike and experience the pleasures of cycling!

Bicycling in Toronto

Bicycles and the TTC

According to Toronto Transit Commission policy, bicycles are allowed on the subway except during rush hours. Monday thru Friday 6:30 a.m. to 9:30 a.m. and 3:30 p.m. to 6:30 p.m. you can't take your bike on the subway. Bicycles are permitted on the subway at all other times. The subway facilitates reaching paths on the other side of town and also useful in case of flat tire, mechanical breakdown or bad weather. Subway stations convenient to each route are indicated in the descriptions and on the accompanying maps.

Cycling safety

When riding on Toronto's streets, whether for shopping, commuting to work, or riding to a bicycle trail, safety should be your first consideration. Always be alert to cars; motorist are not always going to be aware of you. Choose a route that follows streets with the least traffic, avoiding main arteries. Keep to the far right of the road. Groups should always keep in single file. Obey stop signs and traffic lights, even if it means losing your momentum. Watch for parked cars that may suddenly pull in front of you, and for drivers or passengers who may open their car door into your path. If you see a wisp of exhaust coming from a car or if someone is occupying the driver's seat, slow down, check the traffic around you and be prepared to stop or ride around the car.

Be aware of the road directly in front of you, as well as what is happening half a block ahead and beyond to the horizon. Defensive bicycling lets you plan what to do well in advance of a situation so you aren't caught by surprise by a merging road, a pothole, broken glass or a storm sewer that might cause you to fall. If there is a hazard in your path, check the traffic around you to determine if you can safely swerve around it. If you can't, stop and wait for an opening in traffic. If you have to go over a bump, slow down and lift yourself out of your seat; this will prevent your spine from absorbing the shock.

Toronto's streetcar tracks are a special hazard. They can catch your front wheel and throw you onto the street. Before crossing streetcar tracks, make sure there is no traffic and then cross the tracks at as close to a 90 degree angle as possible.

When turning or changing lanes, use hand signals. To indicate a left turn extend your left forearm. Signal a right turn by holding your left forearm vertical at a 90 degree angle to your upper arm. Indicate you are slowing down by turning your left forearm down perpendicular to the rest of your arm. Hand signals should be made at least 30 meters (100 feet) in advance.

Make sure you can be seen at night! Your bicycle should have reflectors on the front and back, fixed to the spokes of both wheels, and also as reflective tape on the bicycle frame. Pedals with built-in reflectors are a good safety device. When riding at night wear light coloured clothing that can be easily reflected in car headlights. Reflective vests are also an excellent idea.

Bicycle lights are not so much intended to light up the road ahead, which they do only minimally, as to make sure that drivers can see you on the road. There are two main types of bicycle lights: battery-powered and generator-driven lights. The generator-driven light has a wheel that revolves against the tire to produce a current which powers the lights. They don't require batteries so you won't be caught with dead batteries and no light, but a generator increases your pedalling resistance and the light shines only when you are moving. As soon as you stop the light goes out.

Leg-lights that attach with a strap to your leg are very effective in attracting motorist's attention because the light beam goes up and down as you pedal.

If you do even a moderate amount of cycling on city streets, consider getting a cycling helmet. They are available at most cycling shops and are well worth their cost. In case of an accident a helmet could easily save your life.

Also available in bicycle shops are the two-meter (six-foot) bicycle flags. As they extend above the height of most traffic and have brightly coloured flags at the top, they can help a motorist to spot you on a busy street and will also stand out on the highway.

Toronto's off-street bikeways free you from worrying about cars, but you still need to watch for and be courteous to people walking along the same paths.

Buying a Bicycle

What kind of bicycle?

The best bicycle to buy is the one that suits your specific needs. If you need a bike only to go to the corner store, a one-speed with coaster brakes is probably sufficient. But if you plan to go cycling often, then a touring bicycle is a good investment.

Ten-speed touring bicycles have a large range between the low and high gears. This allows you to ride steadily up steep hills or pedal against a strong wind and still be able to cruise over level terrain at a good pace. Most touring bikes have dropped handlebars which allow you to ride in a streamlined position, reducing the amount of energy you expend overcoming air resistance. Racing bicycles are similar in appearance to touring bikes but are more fragile and are not meant for riding over regular roads.

The "mountain" or "off-road" bicycles are designed to withstand the rough handling of backcountry dirt roads. They combine the best features of the one-speed coaster-brake bicycle and the 10-speed touring bike. These mountain bikes have fat tires (2½ inches wide), wide range gearing — up to 18 speeds — to get up and down hills, upright handlebars for better control, a wide seat and heavy-duty brakes.

Three-speed and five-speed bicycles are also suitable for day-long tours. Some have dropped handlebars, but most have upright handlebars and spring saddles. If you are not accustomed to the dropped handlebars and hard seat typical of a touring ten-speed, and you don't plan on any long trips, you may find these easier to ride. As well, some ten-speeds are available with upright handlebars and wide seats.

The best place to buy a bicycle is a reputable shop that backs its bikes with a guarantee and has trained mechanics to service bicycles on the premises. In a good bike shop, salesmen are knowledgeable and can help you choose a bike that best fits your needs in your price range. Bike shops usually sell only quality makes. Cheaper brands carried by department and discount stores often don't hold up as well on the road.

Shop around and compare different makes and prices. When you've decided on one, try to purchase it from a shop near your home. Even if it costs a few dollars more, the extra convenience is worth it. When you bike needs adjustments it's much easier to take it a couple of blocks than to haul it across town to the place where you saved a few dollars.

Getting the right size

Buy a bike that fits you properly. Your first consideration is frame size. Standard adult bicycle frames range from 19 to 26 inches. This is the distance between the top of the frame, where the seat post slides into the frame, and the center of the crank, where the pedals revolve. Your frame size is roughly 11 inches shorter than your inseam measurement.

To check for proper frame size, get on the bicycle. With both your feet flat on the ground, you should be able to straddle the top tube of the frame with about two inches to spare. The obsolete way of asking for a bicycle by its wheel size dates from the time when all bicycles were one-speed.

Adjust the saddle to the proper height; you should be able to sit on the seat while one foot is touching the ground. Now get off the bicycle. With your elbow touching the tip of the saddle, the handlebars should not be more than one inch from your fingertips. If the handlebars are too far forward, too low or too high, ask the shop to adjust them. It may be necessary to change the handlebar extension (the piece connecting the handlebars to the stem) for one of a different size. The handlebars should be just a bit lower than the saddle.

All bicycles, except racers, are available in men's or women's models. On women's bicycles the top part of the frame is inclined to allow women to wear skirts when they ride.

Children, especially those getting a first bike, should be able to put both feet on the ground while sitting in the bike's saddle. If the bicycle has hand brakes be sure that the child can reach and apply them easily. The child can learn to keep his balance by pushing himself along and will soon become confident with the bike. If you start a child with training wheels he will not learn to balance and it will take longer for him to learn to ride without the training wheels.

Secondhand bicycles

Ads for used bicycles can be found in daily and weekly newspapers, and on the bulletin boards of supermarkets, universities, laundromats and some bike shops. The old saying that buying a used car is buying someone else's troubles is sometimes true for bicycles, so you have to be careful. Buying a secondhand bicycle is like buying any other mechanical device. If you don't know what you are buying it may end up costing you a lot more than you anticipated.

When looking at a used bicycle the first thing to do is ride it and see how it handles at slow and fast speeds. If it fits you and is comfortable, examine it carefully for mechanical defects.

Look at the frame from the front and back to see if it is straight and the wheels in line. Turn the bike upside down, letting it rest on the seat and handlebars. The wheels should spin freely and be centered between the forks. Spin the wheel and hold a pencil beside the brake shoe to see how much the wheels move from side to side. It should be no more than three millimeters (one eighth inch).

Holding the bike steady, push the wheel firmly from side to side. It should be well secured at the dropouts and should not move. Pluck each of the spokes — they should all be tight and make the same twanging sound.

Turn the pedals. When the wheels spin there shouldn't be any clicking noises. Put on the brakes; the wheels should stop instantly. Brake shoes should hit the rim squarely and release without sticking.

Examine the frame carefully, particularly at the forks and the joints of the frame. Wrinkled paint may indicate the bicycle was in an accident. A fresh paint job may also indicate this.

The pedals should spin freely with little or no sideways play. Cranks should be straight. Bent cranks may also be a sign that the bike was in an accident.

Gears should change smoothly, without slipping and without a clunking sound. Try all gears with the bike upside down and during your test ride.

With the bicycle right side up, put on the front brakes and try to move the handlebars back and forth. If there is a lot of play, the headset (the part that connects the handlebar stem with the frame) may be worn or need adjustment.

Before you actually purchase the bike, bring it into a repair shop and get a professional estimate on how much repairs will cost.

What to take with you

A day of cycling doesn't require a lot of equipment. You'll probably take a filled water bottle or canteen, a picnic lunch and a few basic tools. Here are a few suggestions.

Bags

For your lunch, extra clothes, patch kit and tools you can use a handlebar bag, panniers, day-pack or basket. Handlebar bags attach to the handlebars and most have a clear map pocket so you can follow your route on the map while riding. They're a good size to hold the items needed for a day-long trip.

Panniers are bags that attach to a carrier and hang alongside the wheel. Both front and rear panniers are available. Rear panniers are preferable as front panniers can stiffen steering. Front panniers are useful for the extra capacity you may need on a multi-day tour when you plan to camp out.

Day-packs, belt pouches and fanny packs are also suitable for carrying a lunch, guidebook and tool kit. Day-packs have more room and you can also fit a sweater and poncho into it. The waist strap on a day-pack will keep the load close to your body so it doesn't move around while you're pedalling.

Baskets, made of wire or wicker, are useful for day-long tours and also for carrying groceries. Pannier-style baskets are also available and may be preferable because they put the load over your rear wheels and will not interfere with your steering.

Baby seats

A well made baby seat should be padded and attach securely to the bicycle. The seat you buy should have straps for holding the baby in, and shields on the sides to keep the child's feet away from the spokes of the wheel. A baby seat in the rear is preferred to a front carrier as it keeps the child out of the wind.

Water bottles

Plastic bottles designed for bicyclists come with wire carriers that attach to the bike's frame. Their double caps have a small opening which will let you drink while pedalling. If you don't have this type of bottle, a regular canteen carried with your other gear is suffi- cient.

Tools

Always carry a small tool kit when you head out for a day-long trip. If you don't have the tools you need to fix a flat or some other minor problem you may have a long walk home. You should have a dependable air pump that will inflate you tires hard enough to ride on. Many cheap pumps can't do this, so test before you buy.

A basic kit contains:
Tire patch kit
Spare inner tube
Tire irons
Air pump
Pressure gauge
Screwdriver
Pliers
Bicycle wrenches
Adjustable wrench
Small knife or scissors
Spare bulb and batteries for your lights

Locks

Anytime you leave your bicycle, even for a few minutes, lock it to something secure; a lamp-post, bicycle rack or some other immovable object. Lock the frame and both the front and rear wheels, or if you have quick release wheels lock the frame and rear wheel and take the front wheel with you. If you don't lock your bicycle securely, a bike thief can get away with it in seconds. You've probably spent a fair amount of money on your bicycle, so protect it with a dependable lock.

Use a thick cable or chain and a strong lock, or the chainless and virtually indestructable Citadel or Kryptonite locks which include a guarantee if your bicycle is stolen. Theft insurance for your bicycle can be included in your household policy. Take the receipt to your insurance agent and have it added to your policy.

Germaine Salois

"Society is always taken by surprise at any new example of common sense." —Emerson

1. Martin Goodman Trail

20 km/12 miles

Toronto's entire Lake Ontario shoreline is the route of the Martin Goodman Trail. The gift of *The Toronto Star* to everyone in Toronto on the city's 150th birthday, the Martin Goodman Trail extends from the Humber River in the west to the eastern Beaches near Victoria Park Avenue. The trail goes along sandy beaches and grassy parks, past historic sites, and through Harbourfront and downtown. Seagulls and other waterfowl are in abundance along the trail.

The trail honours former *Star* president and editor-in-chief Martin Goodman, who died of cancer in 1981 at age 46. Goodman was an athlete who worked to improve the quality of life for Toronto residents.

The Martin Goodman Trail incorporated existing paths at the eastern Beaches and at the western Sunnyside beaches. Toronto's first cycling path was built along the eastern Beaches in 1969, as bicycles were banned from the Beaches boardwalk. In the 1970s the city built bicycle trails along Sunnyside beaches in the west. Between these two paths was an 8-km (5-mile) gap from Bathurst Street to Leslie Street. *The Star* connected the trails to form the continuous Martin Goodman Trail route.

START: As the Martin Goodman Trail follows the entire shoreline of Toronto, just look at the maps and choose your starting point.

"To find new things, take the path you took yesterday."
— John Burroughs

NEAREST SUBWAY: Union Station (the southern station of both north-south lines) is near the mid-point of the Martin Goodman Trail. Exit from Union Station to the corner of Front and Bay Streets, go right on Bay Street to Queens Quay. Here is the Martin Goodman Memorial and the trail.

THE ROUTE: The entire route of the Martin Goodman Trail is marked by green and blue signs with a stylized "M," and blue and green lines down the middle of the path.

Sunnyside: Humber River to Bathurst Street

The western portion of the Martin Goodman Trail goes through parks and waterfront promenades along Toronto's western Sunnyside beaches. The trail begins near Lake Shore Boulevard and Windemere Avenue at the southern end of the Humber River Valley bicycle path (tour 7).

Follow the path along the grassy Sunnyside beaches. The breakwater wall in the lake is a resting place for gulls, ducks and other waterfowl. The pyramid-shaped structure with railway tracks is a memorial to Sir Casimir Gzowski, an engineer who helped build the Grand Trunk Railway and the first International Bridge over the Niagara River.

The sign indicating Colborne Lodge Drive leads north under the Gardiner Expressway to High Park (tour 9).

Continuing on the Martin Goodman Trail, you pass the Sunnyside Bathing Pavillion built in 1921, and the Palais Royale Ballroom dating from 1922. Both buildings are from the time when this area was Sunnyside Amusement Park.

The Martin Goodman Trail stays parallel to Lake Shore Boulevard West. Just past the Argonaut Rowing Club the trail follows Aquatic Drive on the lake's edge.

Follow the trail past Ontario Place. On the other side of Lake Shore Boulevard West is Exhibition Place, the site of the Canadian National Exhibition and the Royal Winter Fair.

In Coronation Park you pass a Lancaster Bomber airplane which flew raids over Germany during the Second World War. The trail then follows the sidewalk along Lake Shore Boulevard West past the Tip Top Tailors building dating from 1929, to Bathurst Street.

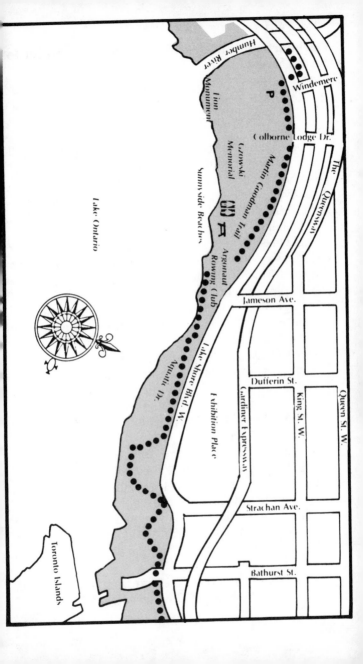

Harbourfront and Downtown: Bathurst Street to Leslie Street

The Harbourfront and downtown section of the Martin Goodman Trail lets you explore the open-air markets and exhibits at Harbourfront and the historic port of Toronto.

From Bathurst Street, the Martin Goodman Trail winds its way behind buildings on the south side of Lake Shore Boulevard West to the intersection of Spadina Avenue and Queens Quay. Here the Martin Goodman Trail is divided into separate paths for bicycling and walking. The bicycling route crosses to the north side of Queens Quay and continues beside the Gardiner Expressway. (The route for walkers in this area follows the south side of Queens Quay).

Ride past the entrance road to the CN Tower. At 554 meters (1,815 feet) the tower is the tallest free-standing structure in the world. At York Street turn south to Queens Quay and continue along the north side of Queens Quay. At Bay Street is the Martin Goodman Memorial. On the south side of Queens Quay are the Toronto Island Ferry Docks (tour 2).

At the foot of Yonge Street is *The Toronto Star* building. The path continues along the south side of Queens Quay East

At Parliament Street, the trail winds along Lake Shore Boulevard East, under the elevated Gardiner Expressway, to Cherry Street. At the intersection of Cherry Street and Lake Shore Boulevard East will be the link with the planned bicycle path along the Lower Don River joining the Martin Goodman Trail with the network of bicycle paths along Bayview, Taylor Creek and Wilket Creek.

Ride south on Cherry Street, crossing the bascule lift bridges over the Keating Channel which is the outlet of

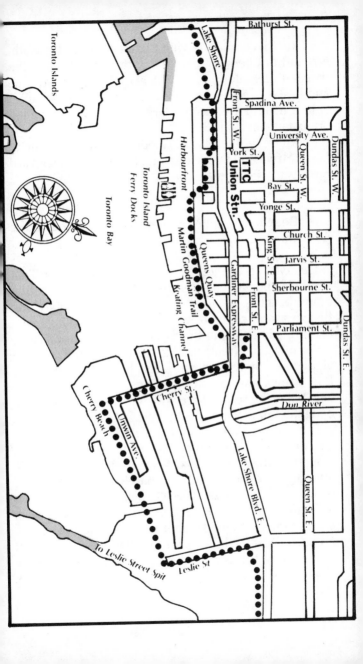

the Don River, and the Ship Channel. From the southern end of Cherry Street, follow the path through the wooded area along Cherry Beach. At Unwin Avenue and Leslie Street is the access road to the Leslie Street Spit, a natural area with a large waterfowl population on its lagoons (tour 3).

Continue on the Martin Goodman Trail north along Leslie Street and then east along Lake Shore Boulevard East to the Beaches.

The Beaches: Leslie Street to Fernwood Park Avenue

The eastern section of the Martin Goodman Trail parallels the famous Beaches boardwalk beside the sandy beaches of Lake Ontario. On a warm day, the Beaches are covered with people picnicking, sunbathing and enjoying the beautiful view of the lake.

From Leslie Street, the Martin Goodman Trail goes along Lake Shore Boulevard East. Ride past Ashbridges Bay, named after Sarah Ashbridge, a widow from Philadelphia who settled here with her two sons and three daughters in 1793.

The Martin Goodman Trail enters Woodbine Park and meanders beside the Beaches boardwalk. On this stretch of the trail you pass the Donald Summerville olympic-sized pool, and the baseball diamonds and paddle ball courts of Kew Gardens. In 1879 Joseph Williams turned his 8-hectare (20-acre) lakeside farm into a park and named it after Kew Gardens in London.

Bicycle past the large oak trees that provide pleasant shade along the easternmost section of the trail. The Martin Goodman Trail ends at Fernwood Park Avenue.

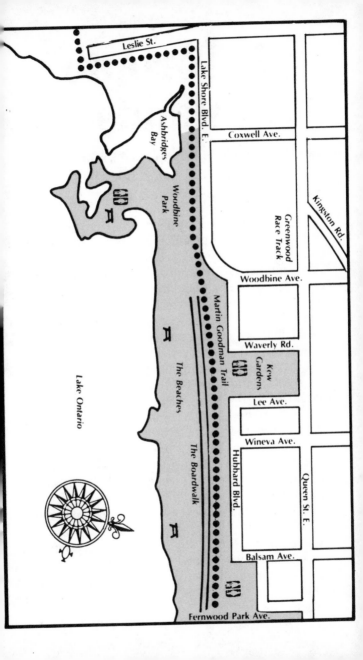

2. Toronto Islands

Ward's to Hanlan's 5.25 km/3.25 miles
Ward's to Centre 3.25 km/2 miles
Centre to Hanlan's 2 km/1.2 miles

Only eight minutes by ferry from downtown, the Toronto Islands are beautiful parkland with abundant birdlife, picnicking areas and peaceful places to enjoy Lake Ontario. With its flat pathways along scenic lagoons, wooded parkland and sandy beaches, the Toronto Islands have long been a cyclist's haven. The first bicycle paths on the Toronto Islands were the work of Ned Hanlan, champion sculler and city alderman for the Islands around the turn of the century.

At that time, the Toronto Islands were largely a summer resort community for residents of the city of Toronto. On Ward's Island, named after fisherman David Ward who settled here in the 1830's, there was a popular tent city. Many people brought tents, stoves, and furniture to camp here for the summer on rented lots. By the mid-1930's cottages replaced the tents. During the housing shortage following World War II summer residents were encouraged to winterize their cottages and live in them year-round. The winterized cottages are still lived in.

On Hanlan's Point, John Hanlan —the father of Ned— built Hanlan's Hotel, one of a number of hotels that were on the Toronto Islands. In the early 1900s Hanlan's Point had a popular amusement centre com-

plete with barkers, vaudeville acts and a merry-go-round. The amusement area was demolished in 1937 to make way for the Toronto Island Airport.

START: Access to the Toronto Islands is by ferry from the docks on Queens Quay at the foot of Bay Street. If you're coming by bicycle, you can take the Martin Goodman Trail (see tour 1). If you're coming by car, there are parking lots along Queens Quay near the ferry docks. During the summer finding a parking space may be difficult.

NEAREST SUBWAY: Union Station (at the southern end of both north-south lines) is the stop for the ferry docks. From the subway station exit onto Front Street and Bay Street. Go right on Bay Street to the ferry docks.

The Great Toronto Bicycling Guide

FERRIES: Ferry service is operated to Ward's Island, Centre Island and Hanlan's Point. On weekends, bicycles are permitted only on the Ward's Island and Hanlan's Point ferries. For a tape recorded message giving current schedules and fares, call (416) 947-8193. Service is seasonal. During the summer there is service to all three points. The ferry to Ward's Island is the only one that operates year round.

THE ROUTE: You can take the ferry to any of the three points. As ferry service to Ward's Island operates year-round, this route begins here.

From the Ward's Island ferry dock, follow the sign "To Boardwalk and Beach," to the boardwalk along Lake Ontario. Go to the right and ride along the wooden boardwalk. The peninsula you see in Lake Ontario is the Leslie Street Spit.

At Centre Island the path is paved. Opposite the concrete pier, is the path across Centre Island to the Centre Island Ferry Dock.

Continue along the lakeshore to the Gibraltar Lighthouse, erected in 1808 and the oldest landmark in Toronto still on its original site. The lighthouse is believed to be haunted by the ghost of J.P. Rademuller, its first keeper who was killed in 1815 by drunken soldiers after he refused to continue giving beer to them. His skeleton was found nearby by James Durnan, keeper of the lighthouse from 1832 to 1852.

Past the lighthouse is a stocked trout pond where you can fish for trout. Stay on the paved path near the lake past the sand dunes and driftwood-strewn beaches, to Hanlan's Point.

You can take the ferry back to the city at the Hanlan's Point Ferry Dock, or return to Centre Island or all the way to Ward's Island.

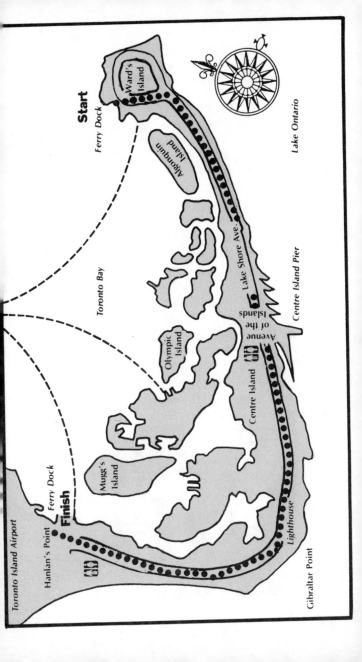

Edward "Ned" Hanlan

The first bicycle paths on the Toronto Islands were one of the less-known accomplishments of sculling champion Ned Hanlan, alderman around the turn of the century and one of the greatest athletes of the 19th century. Hanlan was the first Canadian to win a world championship and became a national hero.

Born in Toronto in 1855, Hanlan moved to the Toronto Islands when his father acquired the Island's popular Hanlan's Hotel. It was said that Ned Hanlan learned to row before he could walk.

In 1873, at age 18, Hanlan became amateur sculling champion of Toronto Bay. In 1876 he turned professional and won the Ontario championship in that year, the Canadian championship in 1877, the American championship in 1878 and the English championship in 1879 where he established a world record on the Tyne. In 1880 he won the world championship on the Thames and retained the title until 1884. Hanlan died in 1908. A statue to his memory stands on the CNE grounds.

Ned Hanlan

3. Leslie Street Spit/Tommy Thompson Park

10 km/6 miles return

A rugged wilderness has grown up on the man-made spit of land that juts 5 km (3 miles) into Lake Ontario from south of Leslie street and extends beyond the eastern end of the Toronto Islands. The paved roadway (cars are prohibited) to the lighthouse at the tip of the peninsula offers very scenic cycling. The peninsula encompasses lagoons, driftwood-strewn shores, and many varieties of plants and wildflowers. The area is known for its excellent birdwatching. The world's largest colony of ring-billed seagulls, as well as sandpipers, terns and a variety of geese and ducks have made the spit's more than 40 hectares (100 acres) of lagoons their home or stopover during migration.

The 189-hectare (466-acre) headland was built as a breakwater for the outer harbour by extensive dredging and a program of land-fill excavated from Toronto's construction sites. In 1985 the spit was named after Metro Toronto's first Parks Commissioner Tommy Thompson who strove to preserve Toronto's natural areas. His "Please Walk on the Grass" signs became well known.

HOURS: Tommy Thompson Park is open weekends and holidays from 9 a.m. to 6 p.m. during spring, summer and fall. To find out about changes to this schedule, call the Metro Toronto and Region Conservation Authority at (416) 661-6600.

START: The roadway begins at the corner of Leslie Street and Unwin Avenue. If you're coming by bike, take the Martin Goodman Trail right to the access road. From the Beaches, the Martin Goodman Trail parallels Lake Shore Boulevard East and turns left onto Leslie Street. From the west, the Martin Goodman Trail goes along Queens Quay and Lake Shore Boulevard East, south along Cherry Street and east on a path parallel to Unwin Avenue to Leslie Street. (See tour 1.)

To get to the spit by car, drive along Lake Shore Boulevard East, which in this area is under the elevated Gardiner Expressway, and turn south down Leslie Street towards the lake. There is parking near the gate to the spit.

NEAREST SUBWAY: From Donlands station (on the Bloor-Danforth line) ride west along Danforth Avenue and go left on Jones Avenue. Follow Jones Avenue to Queen Street East, go left on Queen Street and then right on Leslie Street to the spit.

THE ROUTE: Ride through the gate at the corner of Leslie Street and Unwin Avenue, and onto the roadway along the wilderness headland. After about 1.5 km (1 mile) there is a path on your right which leads to a sandy beach.

The main route continues to the end of the headland where the path climbs to the Toronto Harbour Lighthouse. From here you have a tremendous view of the lagoons on the headland, sailboats cruising on Lake Ontario and the Toronto skyline.

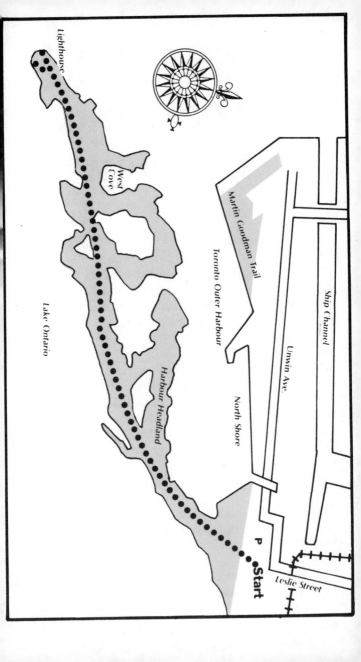

Lighthouse

West Cove

Lake Ontario

Toronto Outer Harbour

Martin Goodman Trail

North Shore

Harbour Headland

Ship Channel

Unwin Ave.

Leslie Street

P •Start

4. Rosedale Valley and Bayview

7 km/4.4 miles

From downtown Toronto, this bikeway takes you along a gently winding route through the wooded Rosedale Valley and along the historic Don River to the Forks of the Don (the junction of the main branches of the Don River). The Rosedale Valley is a natural area situated only a few minutes from Yonge Street.

When Lieutenant-Governor John Graves Simcoe visited the Don River Valley in August 1793, the Don flowed through wide open meadows and Mississauga Indians encamped along its banks. Simcoe named the Don after the Don River in central England. Though the river is now narrower and a large part of the Don Valley is traversed by two major north-south arteries for highway traffic as well as two railway lines, the bicycling path here offers some scenic cycling including sections right along the banks of the Don River.

START: Begin this route at the corner of Yonge Street and Aylmer Avenue outside the Rosedale subway station (on the Yonge Street line).

THE ROUTE: Go east on Aylmer Avenue and follow it until it merges into Rosedale Valley Road. The bicycle

path begins on the right side of the road. The path
winds gradually down through this scenic valley until
you eventually reach Bayview Avenue. Here will be
the junction with the planned bicycle path along the
Lower Don River linking the Bayview path with the
Martin Goodman Trail.

Cross at the traffic lights and go left following the path along the shoulder and in the valley beside the road. You soon go beneath the Bloor Viaduct, opened in 1918 as the Prince Edward Viaduct, which spans the Don Valley and connects Danforth Avenue and Bloor Street. At the time of the Viaduct's construction, a lower deck was included for the track of a future transit system. In 1965 the Bloor-Danforth subway line began operation on this deck.

After going under the Bayview-Bloor Ramp, the path comes out to Bayview Avenue and stays along the shoulder to Pottery Road. Take the Pottery Road exit, cross the bridge over the Don River and turn left immediately. Follow this narrow road along the banks of the Don River. When you reach the Domtar paper mill, go to the right. The path turns off the road just before the Don Valley Parkway bridge and continues between the two fences. Eventually, you reach a junction of several bicycle paths in the Forks of the Don area.

From here you have several options:

— You can return by the same route.

— To the left is a sign reading "Sunnybrook Park 5 km, Edwards Gardens 5 km." That will lead you north to the path through E.T. Seton Park and Wilket Creek Park to Lawrence Avenue East (see tour 5).

— Straight ahead is a sign indicating "Victoria Park Station 5 km, Taylor Creek Park" which will take you east through Taylor Creek Park and Warden Woods (see tour 10).

— To get to the nearest street, follow the signs for Sunnybrook Park and Edwards Gardens, go across the concrete narrow bridge and then over the railway tracks. The wooden steps in front of you lead to Don Mills Road.

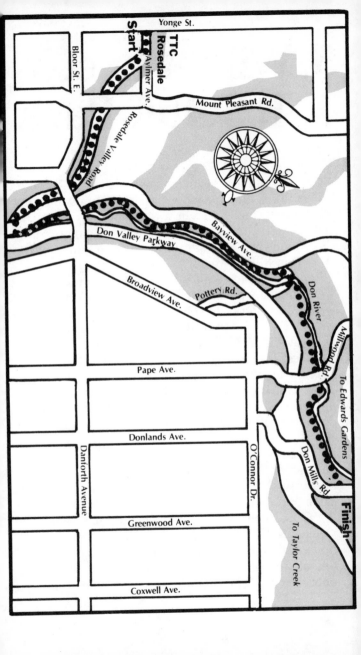

5. Wilket Creek-E.T. Seton Park

5 km/3 miles

One of the most beautiful small valleys in Toronto, Wilket Creek is abundant in birdlife. In spring, bursting wildflowers can be seen near this tributary of the West Don River. This bicycling route goes along Wilket Creek and then through the wide open valley of the West Don River through E.T. Seton Park.

In the late 18th century, the fur traders of the Northwest Company paddled up the West Don River on their way to the interior to collect furs trapped the previous winter. From Toronto, they travelled by boat up the Don River to the Forks of the Don, and then ascended the West Don River to Yonge Street, which had been built by Lieutenant Governor John Graves Simcoe in 1796. Lashing wheels to their boats, they then journeyed north on Yonge Street to the Holland River and continued by water to the trading posts in the Northwest.

E.T. Seton Park is named for the well-known artist and author who was a recognized authority on wildlife in North America. As a boy in the 1870s, Ernest Thompson Seton built a small cabin in the forest near the Don River where he went after school and on weekends. He later used the Don River Valley as a setting for his stories about the adventures and personalities of animals he observed here. The stories were published in 1898 in the bestselling *Wild Animals I*

"To be a discoverer you must go looking for something." —Walter Teller

Have Known, the first of his 40 books. He later moved to the United States where he was chief of the Boy Scouts of America from 1910 to 1915.

START: This path begins in the Edwards Gardens parking lot on Leslie Street just south of Lawrence Avenue East.

NEAREST SUBWAY: From Lawrence station (on the Yonge Street line) go east on Lawrence Avenue East all the way to Leslie Street. Go right on Leslie Street to the Edwards Gardens parking lot.

THE ROUTE: As bicycles are not permitted in Edwards Gardens, it is necessary to lock your bicycle and enjoy the floral displays on foot. After visiting the gardens, take the path from the parking lot on Leslie Street down to the path along Wilket Creek. Go south through Wilket Creek Park. Ride under the Eglinton Avenue East bridge, and the C.P. Railway trestle and enter E.T. Seton Park.

Continue south along the West Don River through E.T. Seton Park. After passing under the Overlea Boulevard bridge, you eventually reach a sign reading: "Edwards Gardens 5 km, Sunnybrook Park 5 km."

From here you have several options:

— You can return by the same route;

— Go left and follow the signs for Taylor Creek to the bicycle paths along Taylor Creek and Warden Woods (see tour 10).

— Go southwest on the bicycle path along Bayview Avenue and then up the Rosedale Valley to Yonge Street and Aylmer Avenue (see tour 4); Follow the signs for Taylor Creek and go under Don Mills Road and over the railway tracks. Turn right to the bicycle bridge under the highway cloverleaf.

— To get to the nearest street, follow the signs for Taylor Creek Park and go along the wooden walkway under Don Mills Road. Don't go right over the railway tracks but up the wooden steps in front of you to Don Mills Road.

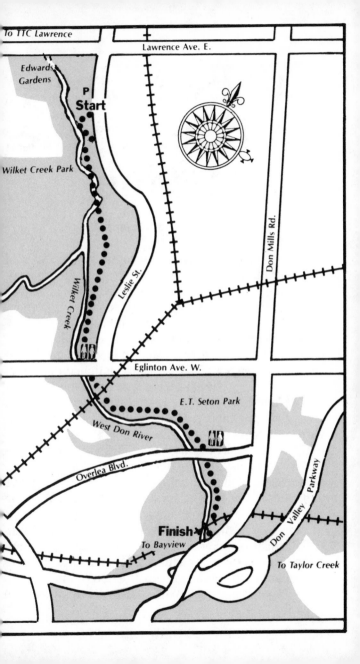

6. Belt Line and Cedarvale Ravine

6 km/4 miles on unpaved surface

During Toronto's real estate boom of the 1880s, a promoter named John Moore built a commuter railway connecting Toronto with the new suburbs of Moore Park and Forest Hill when these areas were first opened for development. Moore's Toronto Belt Line Railway began service in 1892 with six trains per day in each direction. By 1895 the real estate boom had gone bust and the passenger service was discontinued due to insufficient traffic. The rails were later removed. The first part of this bicycling route is on the old Belt Line right-of-way, a tree-lined path running between the backyards of Forest Hill homes.

The second part of this route takes you through the Cedarvale Ravine, where over 30 species of birds including owls, cardinals and finches nest. In the late 1960s and early 1970s the Cedarvale Ravine was part of the proposed route of the Spadina Expressway which was to run south from Highway 401 into downtown Toronto. The plan sparked a lot of controversy, and there were protests by many citizens. In June 1971 the provincial government halted construction of the expressway. Now called the W.R. Allen Expressway, the

John Moore

limited access highway ends at Eglinton Avenue West, several blocks north of the Cedarvale Ravine.

START: Begin this route at the corner of Yonge Street and Chaplin Crescent, outside the Davisville subway station (on the Yonge Street line).

THE ROUTE: Go west on Chaplin Crescent, turn left on Lascelles Boulevard and follow the bicycle path through Oriole Park to the intersection of Frobisher Avenue and the continuation of Lascelles Boulevard.

Opposite the TTC Davisville carhouse yards is the Belt Line right-of-way. Follow the path through Forest Hill. It crosses Oriole Parkway and Avenue Road. After going under the Eglinton Avenue West bridge, the path crosses Bathurst Street.

A wire link fence at the sidewalk beside the W.R. Allen Expressway at the end of the Belt Line right-of-way prevents access, so when you reach Old Park Road turn left. Go right on Ridge Hill Drive to the sidewalk along the Allen Expressway. Turn left and follow the sidewalk to Eglinton Avenue West.

Go right on Eglinton Avenue West and pass the Eglinton West subway station (on the Spadina line). Cross Eglinton Avenue at the traffic lights and go left along Eglinton Avenue to Everden Road. Turn right on Everden Road. At Ava Road and Everden Road is the path through Cedarvale Park and the Cedarvale Ravine. Follow the path through this natural area. It emerges at the Heath Street West entrance to the St. Clair West subway station (on the Spadina line). (Entrance here is by cash or tokens only; the gates aren't large enough to allow entrance with bicycles.)

Turn left on Heath Street West, right on Tweedsmuir and right again onto St. Clair Avenue West. Cross to the south side of St. Clair Avenue at the first traffic lights. On the left side of the entrance to the St. Clair West subway station descend along the trail into the ravine. The path goes under the Spadina Road bridge and eventually emerges at Boulton Drive just south of Russell Hill Road.

From here you can return via the same route. The nearest subway station is Dupont (on the Spadina line). To get to it go right on Boulton Drive to Dupont Street, then right on Dupont Street to Spadina Road and the entrance to the subway station.

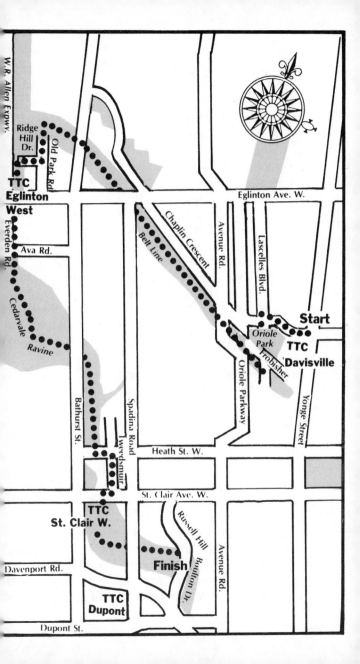

John Moore and the Belt Line

When you explore the old Belt Line path you are following the route of a pioneering effort in rapid transit in Canada. Building the Belt Line Railway was just one aspect of the wide-ranging career of John Moore.

Born in Markham in 1844, Moore moved to Toronto in 1872 and worked as an insurance firm's accountant. In 1881 he led an expedition party west to choose the townsite which became Red Deer, Alberta. To encourage settlers for the new town he wrote *The Homesteader's Guide to Saskatchewan and the Northwest*.

Back in Toronto, Moore was elected to the Yorkville village council. In 1883, when the growing city of Toronto annexed Yorkville, Moore became an alderman on Toronto City Council. In 1884 he served on the committee to plan the 50th anniversary celebrations of Toronto's incorporation in 1834.

During the 1880s Toronto was experiencing a real estate boom. Moore obtained a charter for the Toronto Belt Land Corporation in 1889 for the development of suburbs in present-day Moore Park and the upper village of Forest Hill —the area northwest of Bathurst Street and Eglinton Avenue West. To attract buyers he published a beautifully illustrated brochure depicting the Belt Land properties, and built the Belt Line Railway as a fast and safe way for residents to commute from their suburban homes to work in the city.

The Belt Line Railway started at Union Station and went east to the Don River, north along the Don and then west through what is now the Moore Park Ravine and the Mount Pleasant Cemetery. It crossed Yonge Street on a railway overpass that is still in place. West

FOREST HILL AT BATHURST STREET

The Belt Line near Bathurst Street and Eglinton Avenue West as depicted in Moore's real estate brochure.

of Yonge Street, the Belt Line traversed Forest Hill (the section in this bicycling route). Just past Dufferin Street the route turned south back to Union Station. Four train stations were situated along the route.

When service began in 1892 there were six trains per day in each direction. Only two years later passenger trains were discontinued due to insufficient traffic. The building boom of the 1880s ended in the depression of 1894 and too few people moved to these suburbs to support the service.

After the failure of the Belt Line, Moore moved to Red Deer, Alberta and in 1905 became the first member of the provincial legislature for Red Deer. He also built the Alberta Central Railway connecting Red Deer to the C.P.R. mainline. In 1910 he returned to Toronto. Moore died in 1917 and is buried in the Mount Pleasant Cemetery. In recent years citizens' committees have worked towards protecting the remaining Belt Line right-of-way as a linear park.

7. Humber River Valley

13 km/8 miles one way

The picturesque Humber River Valley is one of Toronto's major river valleys. Once an important transportation route for Indians, explorers, missionaries and fur traders, the Humber is now a scenic wooded route for bicycling and exploring nature. Ducks, seagulls and shorebirds can be seen throughout the route.

Near the mouth of the Humber River, where it flows into Lake Ontario, is the area the Indians gave the name Toronto, meaning "carrying place" or "meeting place." In 1720 the French built a *Magasin Royal* (King's store) on the Humber to encourage the Indians to bring their furs to them, instead of the British trading posts at Oswego or Albany. This post served the Humber for 10 years. The second French post on the Humber, then called the Toronto, was built in 1750 and named Fort Toronto after the river. It was renamed the Humber, after the Humber River in England, by John Graves Simcoe who was the Lieutenant-Governor of Upper Canada (which became the province of Ontario in 1867) from 1791 to 1796.

The end of this bicycling route is near the spot where Hurricane Hazel caused its worst destruction when it hit Toronto on October 15, 1954.

START: This route begins at the western end of the Martin Goodman Trail (see tour 1) at Lake Shore Boule-

The Old Mill circa 1902

vard West and Windemere Avenue. There is parking nearby.

NEAREST SUBWAY: Old Mill station (on the Bloor-Danforth line) is near the route. From the station, go right onto Humber Boulevard and then right again on Old Mill Road to the Old Mill Bridge. You can pick up the bicycle trail here.

THE ROUTE: From Lake Shore Boulevard West and Windemere Avenue, follow the path west along the north side of Lake Shore Boulevard. The path turns north and goes under the Gardiner Expressway and railway tracks. It crosses the Humber River on the sidewalk of The Queensway bridge, then loops under the bridge and goes north through the parkland along the Humber.

The path emerges from the parkland at Stephen Drive opposite Cloverhill Road. Turn right on Stephen Drive to Riverwood Parkway. Turn left on Riverwood Parkway and then right on Humber Valley Road, which leads back into the wooded parkland along the Humber River.

Soon after passing under the Bloor Street bridge, you reach Old Mill Road. On your left is the remains of the

Old Mill built in 1848 of stone quarried from the Humber River Valley. This sawmill and earlier mills on this site supplied lumber used to build the new settlement of York, which became the city of Toronto. The upper floor of this mill was later used for storing apples grown in the nearby orchards. On a cold night in 1891 a fire was lit in the stove to keep the apples from freezing. An overheated stove pipe fell to the floor and the mill was soon a mass of flames.

Turn right and cross the Old Mill Bridge, built in 1916, and continue north on the east side of the Humber River. Just south of the Dundas Street West bridge, the path goes onto Lundy Avenue and then left onto Old Dundas Street and then rejoins the parkland along the river.

After passing under the Dundas Street West bridge, you come to a long footbridge across the Humber River, On the bridge are benches for you to sit and enjoy the view of the river.

Past the bridge, the path goes under a railway trestle and then through a very wooded area to James Gardens. Here are picnic tables and barbecue pits. On the other side of the Humber is a golf course where Black Creek flows into the Humber River. A side-trail a bit farther north leads to washrooms.

The path goes under the Scarlett Road bridge, crosses Eglinton Avenue West and the Eglinton bicycle path (tour 8), and continues north along the Humber River. The trail turns west and ends at the corner of Tilden Crescent and Raymore Drive. It was here that flooding caused by Hurricane Hazel took the lives of 36 residents in 1954.

Return along the same route to Lake Shore Boulevard West and your starting point at the western end of the Martin Goodman Trail.

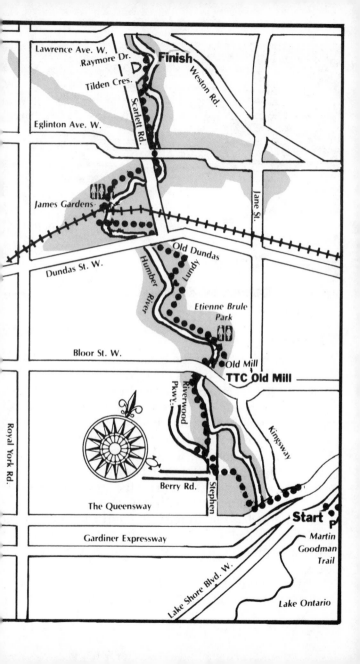

Hurricane Hazel and the Humber

The preservation of the Humber River Valley as natural parkland was one of the legacies of Hurricane Hazel which struck Toronto on October 15, 1954. Hurricane Hazel began off the coast of the Caribbean island of Grenada. It first hit the island of Haiti where it took the lives of over 200 people. Heading north, Hazel battered the east coast of the United States, then moved west and paused briefly over Lake Ontario.

Rain had fallen on Toronto for the previous week and the earth could not absorb any more moisture. Unleashing its fury on Toronto, the hurricane's torrential rainfall flooded all the area's rivers and creeks. The worst destruction was caused by flooding at the Humber.

At Raymore Drive, near the northern end of this bicycle route, a bridge tore loose and fell into the river.

Debris flowing downstream piled against the bridge, partly damming the river and diverting the flood-water down Raymore Drive. Within an hour the fourteen old houses built on posts and pilings on the lower section of Raymore Drive were washed away with many of their occupants. Hearing cries for help, local firemen tied ropes around their waists and tried to swim out to the victims, but the current was too strong. They were helpless as the cries grew weaker and the victim's bodies were washed downstream.

Hurricane Hazel caused the deaths of 81 people in the Toronto area. Thousands lost their homes. In the years following the hurricane, the Toronto and Region Conservation Authority acquired land in the valley of the Humber, and Toronto's other rivers and creeks, as part of their flood control master plan. One of the benefits of this master plan has been the preservation of this scenic natural area along the Humber River for future generations.

8. Mimico Creek

21 km/13 miles

The Indians called the area around Mimico Creek Omimeca, meaning "the resting place of wild pigeons." This area is now the borough of Etobicoke, another Indian name, which means "the place where the black alders grow." Bicycle paths through parkland along Mimico Creek and along Eglinton Avenue West can be linked with the Humber River Valley bicycle path to form a circuit route.

Along this route is Montgomery's Inn, believed to be the oldest public building in Etobicoke. Around 1820 when this area was being settled for farming, Irish-born Thomas Montgomery set up a small log tavern near Mimico Creek. Business was good and in 1832 he built the inn on Dundas Street, a main highway at that time. The inn was a popular stopping place for travellers and for farmers transporting their grain along Dundas Street to the mills on the Humber River. It's an interesting stop for cyclists along this route.

START: At the southwest corner of Eglinton Avenue West and Jane Street is the eastern end of the Eglinton bicycle path. On the other three corners of this intersection is Eglinton Flats Park with open fields and picnic tables.

NEAREST SUBWAY: Old Mill subway station (on the Bloor-Danforth line) is along this bicycling route. If you want to come by subway, start this circuit tour from the Old Mill station. From the station, go right on Humber Boulevard, right again on Old Mill Road to the Old Mill Bridge and then go left onto the Humber River Valley part of this route.

THE ROUTE: From Eglinton Avenue West and Jane Street, follow the Eglinton bicycle path west across the bridge over the Humber River. At the intersection of Scarlett Road, the Eglinton bicycle path crosses the Humber River Valley bicycle path. This is where this circuit route will end.

Montgomery's Inn

Continue west on the Eglinton path until you reach Mimico Creek. It's situated west of Martin Grove Road and east of The East Mall and Highway 427. (The Eglinton bicycle path continues west parallel to Eglinton Avenue West to Renforth Drive and then along a Hydro right-of-way into Centennial Park near the border with Mississauga.)

Ride south on the bicycle path along Mimico Creek through West Deane Park and under the Martin Grove bridge and the Rathburn Road bridge. At the end of the path, carry your bike up the stairs to Kipling Avenue. Go right on Kipling Avenue and then left at the first traffic lights onto Burnhamthorpe Road. Turn left onto Dundas street and right on Montgomery Road. At this corner is the Montgomery Inn, an example of 19th century Loyalist Georgian architecture. It's open Monday to Friday from 9:30 a.m. to 4:30 p.m., and Saturdays and Sundays from 1 p.m. to 5 p.m. Tea is served daily from 2 p.m. to 4:30 p.m.

Go down Montgomery Road and turn left at Belvedere Boulevard opposite the Central Park Etobicoke Memorial Pool and Health Club. At Royal York Road continue on King George Road. Go right on The Kingsway and left onto Old Mill Road which joins Bloor Street West at the same point as the Kingsway. Ride along Old Mill Road. (Old Mill subway station is to your right on Humber Boulevard.)

Cross the Old Mill Bridge and then follow the Humber River Valley path on the left. The path goes north, under the Dundas Street West bridge, crosses a footbridge over the Humber River and continues along the west side of the Humber to Eglinton Avenue West and Scarlett Road near the starting point of this tour. (See tour 7 for historical details on the Humber River Valley.)

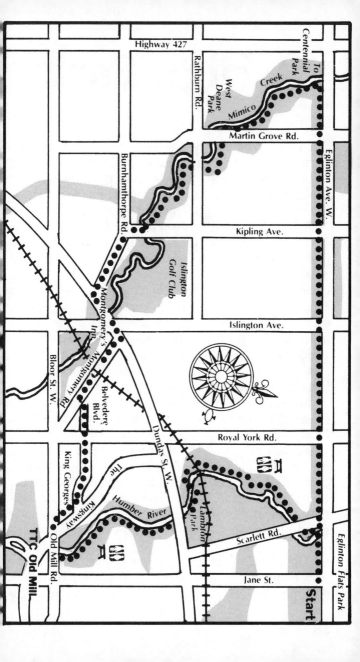

9. High Park

A popular natural respite close to downtown, 137-hectare (300-acre) High Park offers scenic cycling through forests, along the shores of natural Grenadier Pond, past historic sites and through a small zoo. Picnic facilities are found throughout the park.

High Park was the estate of architect and city-surveyor John Howard. In 1836 he purchased 67 hectares (165 acres) here and called the property High Park as it rose several hundred feet above Lake Ontario. Howard cleared some of the forest and built paths and roads. In 1873 he donated High Park to Toronto as a public park on the condition that alcoholic beverages never be sold in the park. The rule is still enforce. Howard's home, which he called Colborne Lodge, is now a museum.

In 1876, on Howard's advice, the city acquired 70 hectares (172 acres) adjoining the park to the east. The 29 hectares (71 acres) to the west, including 14-hectare (35-acre) Grenadier Pond, was bought by the city in 1930.

Grenadier Pond is named for the British soldiers who used to drill on its frozen surface during the mid-19th century. Many species of waterfowl can be seen year round on the pond. During spring and autumn migrations many ducks, seagulls, geese, grebes and swallows stop in the park.

START: Begin your explorations of High Park at the park entrance on Bloor Street West opposite High Park Avenue. The park's roads are closed to cars on weekends and holidays from May to September. If you're coming by car during those periods, park along Bloor Street West or High Park Avenue.

NEAREST SUBWAY: High Park station (on the Bloor-Danforth line) is beside the park. Exit from the station onto High Park Avenue. Go to the right on High Park Avenue and cross Bloor Street West to the entrance of High Park.

THE ROUTE: Wander the network of interconnecting park roads and paths. Especially scenic is the route followed by the High Park trackless train which skirts the shores of Grenadier Pond and other waterways. Cars are not permitted on this route at any time.

Some of High Park's attractions that you might want to explore are:

Colborne Lodge: John Howard named his home after Sir John Colborne, Lieutenant Governor of Ontario. It is now a museum containing original furnishings, including the kitchen and fireplace, and examples of early Canadian art. It's open Monday to Saturday from 9:30 a.m. to 5 p.m., and Sundays and holidays from 12 noon to 3 p.m.

Tomb: In 1874 Howard erected this tomb for himself and his wife Jemima. It is enclosed by an iron railing that Howard bought from St. Paul's Cathedral in London. When the ship bringing the railing from England sank in Montreal harbour, Howard hired a diver to bring the railing up.

Grenadier Pond: Many birds can be seen here. You can also fish from the shore or from a rented row-boat.

Bandstand: During the summer, Sunday afternoon concerts are performed on this bandstand near Grenadier Pond.

High Park Zoo: Some of the animals in this modest zoo include deer, bison, yaks, llamas, mouflon, sheep, deer, peacocks, rabbits, pheasants and raccoons.

Hillside Gardens: Here you can see hanging gardens, primly trimmed hedges surrounding pools and rose gardens.

Sculpture Symposium Area: The abstract sculptures here were commissioned as a 1967 Centennial project.

Bird Sanctuary: This area is off-limits to visitors.

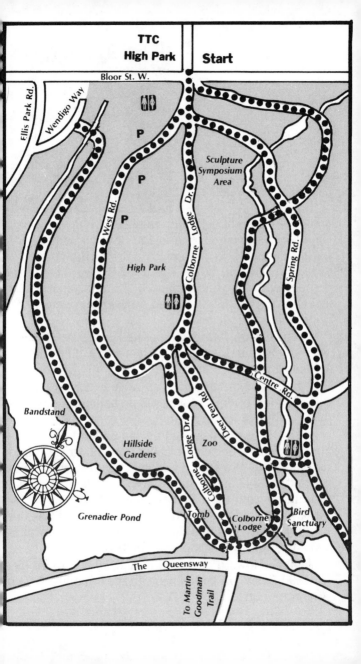

John Howard

Surveyor, architect and engineer John Howard, played a conspicuous role in the development of Toronto in addition to giving High Park to the city.

Born in London, England in 1803, Howard came to Toronto with his wife Jemima in 1832. After a harsh first winter, Howard was hired as a drawing master at Upper Canada College

When Toronto was incorporated in 1834, Howard was made city-surveyor by Toronto's first mayor William Lyon Mackenzie.

During his long career as an architect, Howard designed many bridges, stores, public buildings and residences, though few remain.

In 1843 Howard designed a wing added to Osgoode Hall of the Law Society of Upper Canada. Howard also designed the Provincial Lunatic Asylum which was opened in 1848 and in its day was considered a model institution. Until then, the mentally unbalanced in Ontario were confined to county jails. By the mid-20th century the asylum had slipped below modern hospital standards and was demolished in 1976.

Jemima Howard died in 1877 and John Howard died in 1890. They are buried beneath the tomb just west of Colbrone Lodge.

10. Warden Woods and Taylor Creek

7.5 km/4.5 miles

One of the tributaries of the Don River, Taylor Creek flows westward through scenic Warden Woods and Taylor Creek parks and joins the Don River at the Forks of the Don. At the western end of Taylor creek Park, also known as Taylor's Bush Park, were the farm and apple orchards of a family named Taylor. This bicycle route goes through the country-like wooded valleys and wild fields of Taylor Creek and Warden Woods where more than 200 species of birds have been observed.

START: The path begins at the southwest corner of Warden Avenue and St. Clair Avenue East, opposite the Warden subway station (on the Bloor-Danforth line).

The western end of this route is beside the Don Valley Parkway. To get there by car: Take the Don Valley Parkway and exit for Don Mills Road North. Keep to the right on the curve of the cloverleaf and take the first exit on the right marked "Taylor Creek Park." Follow the road under the Parkway to the parking lot. You can pick up the path here.

THE ROUTE: At Warden Avenue and St. Clair Avenue East is a sign reading "Welcome to Warden Woods." Descend the path beside the sign into the ravine to signs indicating "Taylor Creek Park 2½ km. Victoria Park Station 2½ km." Follow the path along the creek through Warden Woods.

You eventually reach Pharmacy Avenue. Turn right onto Pharmacy Avenue and left on Dolphin Drive. Follow Dolphin Drive to Victoria Park Avenue. (Going left on Victoria Park Avenue will take you to Victoria Park subway station on the Bloor-Danforth line.)

Cross Victoria Park Avenue to the path through Taylor Creek Park. Ride down the hill and along Taylor Creek. After going under the Dawes Road bridge and across a wooden footbridge, you come to an area of picnic tables and barbecue pits.

Continue along the path. Just before the O'Connor Drive bridge is a water fountain and public washrooms. You soon reach parking lots near the junction of the main tributaries of the Don River.

From here you have several choices:

— You can return via the same route.

— You can go north through E.T. Seton Park and along Wilket Creek to Edwards Gardens at Lawrence Avenue East and Leslie Street: Follow the signs indicating Edwards Gardens (see tour 5).

— Go south on the bicycle path along Bayview Avenue and up the Rosedale Valley to Yonge Street and Aylmer Avenue (see tour 4).

— To get to the nearest street, follow the signs for Edwards Gardens and Sunnybrook Park and go across the arched concrete bridge. Climb the hill, cross the wooden bridge over the railway tracks, and go up the wooden steps to Don Mills Road.

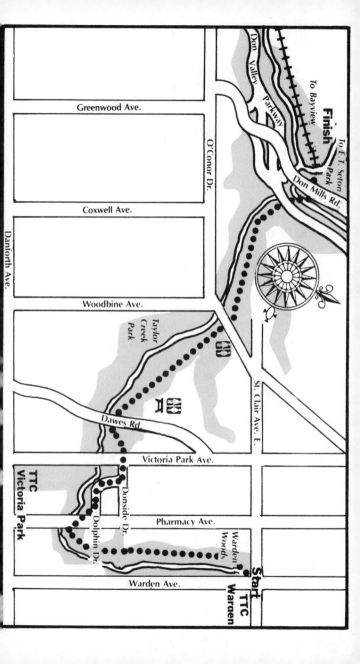

11. Highland Creek

14 km/9 miles

Highland Creek meanders through a wooded and rural valley through Scarborough. It was following an Indian path along Highland Creek that brought David Thomson, a Scot who immigrated to Upper Canada in 1796, to his 162-hectare (400-acre) grant and so became the first European to settle in Scarborough township. Thomson later built a sawmill on Highland Creek, which was supplied with wood by the large stands of pine and hardwood trees along the creek.

Beginning in the 1830s large numbers of settlers arrived to farm in Scarborough. Remnants of a few farms still remain, and parts of this bicycle route along the banks of Highland Creek still reflect a rural character.

START: This route begins at Birkdale Ravine on Ellesmere Road near Birkdale Road just east of Midland Avenue.

NEAREST SUBWAY: From Kennedy Station (on the Bloor-Danforth line), ride the Scarborough Rapid Transit line to Ellesmere station. Exit and go east on Ellesmere Road to the Birkdale Ravine.

THE ROUTE: At Birkdale Ravine follow the "Bike Path" sign with the logo of a yellow heart. After 1.2 km (¾ mile) in the ravine you reach Brimley Road. Go right. Cross Brimley at the traffic lights and continue into Thomson Memorial Park, named after David and Mary Thomson, the earliest settlers of Scarborough township.

You soon reach the Cornell House Museum, originally built in 1850 by William Cornells, one of the early settlers in the township. The museum is open every day during the summer, and on weekends during spring and autumn.

Past the museum you ride through a scenic area with picnic tables. The path goes under the McCowan Road bridge, the Lawrence Avenue East bridge and the Bellamy Road bridge. The Heart Trail section of this route ends in Cedarbrook Park at East Park Boulevard and Markham Road.

"People love bypaths." —Tao Te Ching

From here turn left on Markham Road and then right on Lawrence Avenue East. At Orton Park Road, cross Lawrence Avenue at the traffic lights and continue east on the north side of Lawrence Avenue (walk your bicycle on the sidewalk here as you're going against the traffic flow), crossing a bridge over Highland Creek. (Be sure to cross Lawrence Avenue at Orton Park Road and not near the earlier bridge over a tributary of Highland Creek.)

Just past the bridge, a path leads down to the bicycle path along Highland Creek. Ride the path through the wooded area along Highland Creek into Morningside Park. There are picnic tables and washroom facilities here.

The path continues under the Morningside Avenue bridge. You soon are in a rural area and pass a cow barn. After passing under the Old Kingston Road bridge the route curves up to the south side of Old Kingston Road. Go right, across the bridge over Highland Creek. The path continues along the east side of the creek and soon connects with the road through Highland Creek Park. The park is a good destination for a picnic lunch. Along the park road are washrooms, public telephones and picnic tables. From the end of the road you can lock your bike and walk along the dirt path that continues south along the banks of Highland Creek.

GETTING BACK: You can retrace your route. Or, the quickest route back to Kennedy subway station is to follow the park road to Colonel Danforth Trail and Kingston Road, go left on Kingston Road, and then go right on Lawrence Avenue East to Lawrence East station (on the Scarborough Rapid Transit line). Ride the Scarborough Rapid Transit to Kennedy station.

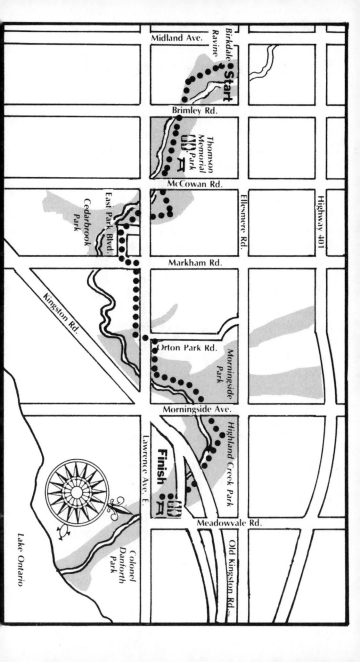

Scarborough's first settler

When Scottish stone mason David Thomson arrived in Canada in 1796, he planned to live in Niagara-on-the-Lake, but moved to Toronto to work on building the parliament building for the new capital. Located near King and Parliament Streets, the building was destroyed during the War of 1812.

Thomson wanted to live outside the city because of his wife's health. After making inquiries, Thomson was directed to the new township of Scarborough, named by Lieutenant Governor John Graves Simcoe and his wife because the bluffs here reminded them of the cliffs at the North Sea resort of Scarborough, Yorkshire.

While choosing a homestead, Thomson found the land beside the lake too sandy for farming so he journeyed north along Highland Creek to more fertile land. He then brought his wife Mary and four children and built a large log cabin here.

At first David Thomson worked in town during the week and returned to his family every Sunday. Life was difficult for the pioneers. Wild animals often tried to steal their livestock. Conditions gradually improved and by 1805 there were more than 100 settlers in Scarborough, most of them Thomsons.

During the War of 1812, David Thomson was captain of the Scarborough militia and served under General Brock. When David Thomson died at age 74, he and his wife had 200 descendants in Scarborough. David and Mary Thomson are buried in St. Andrew's Cemetery on a hill overlooking Thomson Memorial Park.

12. Around the Metro Zoo

10 km/6.5 miles

The Metro Toronto Zoo is nestled in the wide wooded Rouge River Valley on the eastern edge of Toronto. Surrounding the 285-hectare (700-acre) zoo is a bicycle path on its eastern side, and peaceful country roads through rural land on its northern and western sides. This cycling route is a circuit through the scenic natural area that encircles the Metro Zoo.

The Rouge River was an access route for early settlers in the valley. In the 1840s, when the area was first being settled, homesteaders travelled by boat up the Rouge River to their land. Some of the farms along this route were cleared during that period.

START: This route begins at the zoo entrance which is located on Meadowvale Road, north of Sheppard Avenue East. To get there by car, take Highway 401 east, exit onto Meadowvale Road and follow the signs north to the zoo. You can leave your car in the zoo's parking lot.

NEAREST SUBWAY: From Kennedy station (on the Bloor-Danforth line), take the Scarborough Rapid Transit line to McCowan station. Exit onto McCowan Road and ride north on McCowan to Sheppard Avenue East. Go right on Sheppard to Meadowvale Road and then left onto the zoo bicycling path along Meadowvale Road to the entrance of the Metro Zoo.

THE ROUTE: From outside the zoo entrance, ride north on the Metro Zoo bicycle path along the zoo's eastern perimeter. At Finch Avenue East, go left and bicycle on this country road through farmland. Many of the barns here are now used by the zoo. Just past the junction with Reesor Road, the road parallels the Rouge River and then crosses the river on a one-lane metal bridge. Past the bridge the scenery changes from farmland to forest. Go left on Sewells Road which merges back onto Finch Avenue East. To your right is the Morningside Golf Course.

Turn left at Littles Road and ride south through a wooded area. At the railway tracks keep left. From here you can see where suburbs meet the countryside. Littles Road becomes Morningside Avenue here. Continue south to Sheppard Avenue East. Turn left on Sheppard and ride back to Meadowvale Road. Here you rejoin the Metro Zoo bicycle path and ride north to the zoo entrance, your starting point. If you want to visit the zoo, you can lock your bicycle on the bike racks near the entrance.

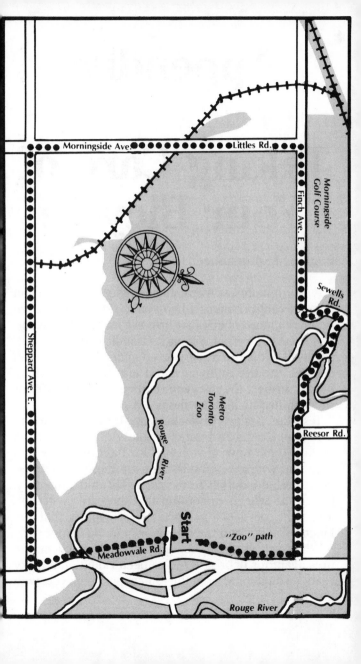

Appendix:

Taking Care of Your Bicycle

Regular Maintenance

A few minutes of maintenance before each trip can help prevent problems when you're riding. With a tire pressure gauge, check that tires are inflated to the correct pressure. Pressure capacity is indicated on the outside wall of the tire. Riding on an underinflated tire can damage the tire and rim and it also makes pedalling harder. Inspect the tires and remove any glass, wire or small stones sticking in them.

Test the brakes to make sure they are working properly. Examine the brake cables: If they are frayed replace them now. If you wait for them to break you may find yourself riding home with one or no brakes. Make sure the derailleur or other gear shifts smoothly. Check the wheels to confirm that they are in straight and tight, particularly quick-release wheels that are taken off often and may have become off-center.

When you get back home from your trip check the tires again for debris. If you've been riding on a dusty road, through mud or in the rain, wipe the bicycle with a cloth.

74

Every so often, depending how much you cycle, go over your bicycle more thoroughly. Make sure all the screws, nuts and bolts are tight or properly adjusted. Examine the brake shoes. If they are very worn, replace them. If they aren't hitting the rim in the right place they should be adjusted. Check for loose or broken spokes. Make sure there is no play in the wheel.

Pedals should spin freely. If you have rubber pedals and they are very worn, replace them. Fraying handlebar grips or loose handlebar tape should also be replaced.

If you ride a three-speed bicycle with an internal gearshift, oil it several times each season with three-speed oil or mineral oil. Don't use all-purpose oil. Make sure the gear cable is properly adjusted or the gears may be damaged.

Flat Tires

The most common problem encountered by bicyclists, a flat tire should not delay you by the side of the path for long. When you feel your tire going flat, get off the bike as soon as possible. Riding on a flat tire can damage the tire, tube and rim.

Before you take the wheel off, check the valve to see if that is where the leak is. Put a drop of spit over the valve: If it bubbles, the problem is a loose valve. Tighten the valve with the valve cap and reinflate the tire.

If the valve isn't the problem then you'll have to disassemble the wheel. Remove the wheel by loosening the nuts or by the quick-release hubs. Using one tire iron at a time, insert it between the tire and the rim and gradually pry the tire loose. Hook the end of the tire iron onto a spoke to hold the tire off the rim while you place the second iron. Be careful not to damage the inner tube. Never use screwdrivers — they may rip the tube. Remove the tire from only one side of the rim.

Remove any nails or other sharp objects that may have punctured the inner tube. Unscrew the nut holding the valve and take out the inner tube.

If it was a loud blow-out then it's probably necessary to replace the tube. If you're not carrying an extra tube you may be able to patch the punctured one so that you can ride home.

Even if it's a small puncture it's quicker to just change the tube and continue on your way. You can repair the tube in the comfort of your home and use it as a spare on subsequent trips.

To repair a punctured inner tube, inflate the tube and pass it near your ear. If you can hear where the air is escaping, circle the hole with a pencil or chalk. If you can't hear or feel where the air is escaping immerse the tube in water and look for escaping bubbles. When you've located the puncture, dry the tube and mark the hole.

With the sandpaper which you will find in your patch kit, rough up the area around the puncture. Spread a layer of glue on this area and let it dry until tacky. Cut the patch so it's the right size, peel off the backing, press it firmly over the hole and let it set for a few minutes.

If the puncture was on the side of the tube touching the rim (the same side of the tube as the valve), it may have been caused by a protruding spoke which should be filed flush. If the tire was cut or cracked, replace it as soon as possible.

To install the inner tube, inflate it slightly and slip the valve stem through its hole on the rim and secure it with the nut. Slip the rest of the tube into the tire, and, using your hands, work the tire gently over the rim. The last six inches or so will be difficult and you'll probably need to use tire irons.

Fit the repaired wheel into the drop-outs and tighten the nuts. For quick-release hubs center the wheel between the forks and push the lever towards the frame. Make sure that it's tight. Now continue your trip!

THE COMPLETE GUIDE TO BICYCLING IN CANADA

Pick up this book and explore some of its over one hundred bicycle touring routes for a day, weekend, week, month or longer in every province in Canada or across Canada. THE COMPLETE GUIDE TO BICYCLING IN CANADA tells you how to get ready for a bicycle trip and guides you along each route with maps and information on road conditions, distances, attractions, weather, camping and accommodation.

240 pages (Published by Doubleday) $12.95

THE COMPLETE GUIDE TO BACKPACKING IN CANADA

For walkers and hikers! THE COMPLETE GUIDE TO BACK-PACKING IN CANADA is the only book that covers the vast resources Canada's national and provincial parks and wilderness areas offer you. Details on the topography, climate, wildlife, the length of trails, and shelters of the hikes in every province and territory, as well as special sections on hiking with children, finding your way, tips on equipment, insects and winter hiking are included.

264 pages (Published by Doubleday) $12.95

GREAT COUNTRY WALKS AROUND TORONTO

Put on comfortable shoes, pick up this book and walk Toronto's most scenic country walking trails! Unknown to many, but within easy reach of everyone in Toronto, are scenic trails for walking, running, birdwatching, exploring with children, picnics and cross-country skiing. The first guide to these walks, pocket-sized GREAT COUNTRY WALKS AROUND TORONTO has maps and drawings, and details on reaching the walks by TTC public transit and by car, the route and how to get back.

64 pages (Published by Great North Books) $2.95

THE GREAT TORONTO BICYCLING GUIDE

Order additional copies of this guide to enjoying scenic and safe cycling in Toronto for friends and relatives for every occasion.

80 pages (Published by Great North Books) $3.95

MORE BOOKS
TO ENJOY THE OUTDOORS!
BY ELLIOTT KATZ

*Available at your favourite bookseller or
direct by mail.*
